AF322621

Table of Contents

What is giving

Luke 6:38 (KJV)

Give, and **it** shall be given unto you; good measure, pressed down, and shaken together, and running over, shall men give into your bosom. For with the same measure that ye mete withal it shall be measured to you again

Giving is a never-ending cycle. Everything you do, you are giving. It is a continual choice on what you are giving.

Deuteronomy 30:19 (NASB)

 I call heaven and earth to witness against you today, that I have placed before you life and death, the blessing, and the curse. So, choose life in order that you may live, you and your descendants,

You can spend all your time giving blessing, health, life, prosperity, and healing. Or you can spend your time giving curses, death, lack, and sickness. It all depends on what comes out of your mouth.

Proverbs 18:21 (KJV)

Death and life are in the power of the tongue, and those who love it will eat its fruit.

We must pay very close attention to what we watch, what we hear, and what we see.

Matthew 12:34-37 (KJV)

O generation of vipers, how can ye, being evil, speak good things? for out of the abundance of the heart the mouth speaketh.

[35] A good man out of the good treasure of the heart bringeth forth good things: and an evil man out of the evil treasure bringeth forth evil things.

[36] But I say unto you, that every idle word that men shall speak, they shall give account thereof in the day of judgment.

[37] For by thy words thou shalt be justified, and by thy words thou shalt be condemned.

Something that God gave me to realize what this is talking about. **Garbage in, garbage out. God in God out.** If we want to continually live in the blessings of God, then we need to focus on more of Him and less of the world around us.

The more you focus on the things of the world, the more you will keep saying the things of the world. The more you focus on God and His word, the more you will speak His word and His blessings over every area of your life.

Some people wonder why they do not have any friends, but they don't take the time to try and reach out to others and build any relationships. They think that people will just magically come up to them and start building friendships.

It all has to do with what you are willing to give so that you can receive what you expect.

Give time to God and He will give time to you. Give time to others and they in turn will give time to you. Give love, receive love, give peace, receive peace, give anger, receive anger, give violence, receive violence, give doubt and unbelief, receive doubt and unbelief.

The only way you are going to be able to give the good things in life is by keeping close observation to what you hear, see, and speak. The thoughts that rule your daily life are a result of what you are feeding your brain on a regular basis. Thoughts turn into words. Words turn into actions. Actions will rule your life.

2 Corinthians 10:3-5 (KJV)

[3] For though we walk in the flesh, we do not war after the flesh:

[4] (For the weapons of our warfare are not carnal, but mighty through God to the pulling down of strong holds;)

[5] Casting down imaginations, and every high thing that exalteth itself against the knowledge of God and bringing into captivity every thought to the obedience of Christ.

Just because your brain thinks something, doesn't mean you have to dwell on it or say it.

In summary,

It does matter what you watch, what you listen to, and what you see. All these things get into your spirit and what you are putting in is what is going to come out.

2. Giving peace

Luke 6:38 (KJV)

Give, and **it** shall be given unto you; good measure, pressed down, and shaken together, and running over, shall men give into your bosom. For with the same measure that ye mete withal it shall be measured to you again.

John 14:27 (KJV)

[27] Peace I leave with you, my peace I give unto you: not as the world giveth, give I unto you. Let not your heart be troubled, neither let it be afraid.

Fear is the opposite of peace. When we go through life, we have the choice to believe the Word, or the world. Any situation can be a struggle or it can be easy and peaceful. We have to learn to approach others that are struggling through a situation to show love, peace, confidence, strength, encouragement, wisdom, or joy. All of these answers to a situation lead to peace in the moment. There are times when others around us are angry. We can take that chance to offer encouragement and wisdom, therefore bringing that person back to a calm, peaceful state of mind and spirit.

Proverbs 15:1(KJV)

 A soft answer turneth away wrath: but grievous words stir up anger.

It is all in the way we approach the situation. Giving peace to a situation brings calmness and quiet. The individual is no longer stressed out and mad but happy and joyful. Giving Godly wisdom and understanding to a person in need will bring about a peaceful situation as long as the individual you are ministering to is willing to accept the wisdom you are trying to impart. There are those that no matter how hard you try to bring peace, they keep rejecting what you are saying. At that point the only thing we can do for that person is

pray and let God put others in their path
that may be able to give possibly the
same answer in a different way so the
individual finally accepts what God is
offering and moves to a peaceful state
of mind.

3. Giving love

Luke 6:38 (KJV)

Give, and **it** shall be given unto you; good measure, pressed down, and shaken together, and running over, shall men give into your bosom. For with the same measure that ye mete withal it shall be measured to you again.

Giving love can come in many different forms.   It can be hope, kindness, compassion, understanding, reassurance, counsel, comfort, sharing, caring, forgiveness, just to name a few.

1 Corinthians 13:13 And now abideth faith, hope, love, these three; but the greatest of these is love.

Ephesians 4:32 And be ye kind one to another, tenderhearted, forgiving one another, even as God for Christ's sake hath forgiven you.

1 Peter 5:7 Casting all your care upon him; for he careth for you.

Even when someone is angry, we can respond with love.

Proverbs 15:1 A soft answer turneth away wrath: but grievous words stir up anger.

In every situation there is a choice to sow love or discord. We need to make sure it is always love. The Christian faith is founded on love.

John 3:16 For God so loved the world, that he gave his only begotten Son, that whosoever believeth in him should not perish, but have everlasting life.

Love is one of the most important attributes we have to have in our Christian walk.

Ephesians 5:1-2

1. Be ye therefore followers of God, as dear children;

2. And walk in love as Christ also
hath loved us and hath given
himself for us an offering and a
sacrifice to God for a sweet
smelling savor.

4. Giving joy

Luke 6:38 (KJV)

Give, and **it** shall be given unto you; good measure, pressed down, and shaken together, and running over, shall men give into your bosom. For with the same measure that ye mete withal it shall be measured to you again.

Psalm 51:12 Restore unto me the joy of thy salvation; and uphold me with thy free spirit.

We are put on this earth to give joy to each other. When someone is sad, we give them encouragement to bring joy back into their life. Joy is a very strong emotion that can get people through a lot of situations. The devil tries to steal our joy so he can get us into things like doubt and unbelief.

Nehemiah 8:10 Then he said unto them, Go your way, eat the fat, and drink the sweet, and send portions unto them for whom nothing is prepared: for this day is holy unto our Lord: neither be ye sorry; for the joy of the Lord is your strength.

Joy can bring strength and peace to every situation. Let everything you do bring joy and gladness to other people that surround you. Joy is contagious. If you are always joyful, then those around you will become joyful and feed off of that emotion.

Psalm 23:6 (KJV)

Surely goodness and mercy shall follow me all the days of my life: and I will dwell in the house of the Lord for ever.

Goodness and mercy lead to a joyful and confident life.

John 10:10 (KJV)

The thief cometh not, but for to steal, and to kill, and to destroy: I am come that they might have life, and that they might have it more abundantly.

Abundant life leads to a joyful and peaceful life. Every time we meet someone, whether it be someone we know or someone new, we have the opportunity to spread different emotions. We have to be careful what emotion we are showing. In those times where you have had a hard day and you seem to be in not a good mood, you need to have someone in your life that you can turn to and share with so you can get your joy back.

5. Giving doubt and unbelief

Luke 6:38 Give, and **it** shall be given unto you; good measure, pressed down, and shaken together, and running over, shall men give into your bosom. For with the same measure that ye mete withal it shall be measured to you again.

Doubt and unbelief are 2 major causes in most failures. We don't believe we can do something and therefore we can't. We think about doing something and then doubt comes in. You feel like you don't have the skills or education to complete the task at hand. People in this situation are very easy to influence in the wrong direction. We can tell someone "I don't think so" and that can be the biggest start to a very significant failure.

Any time we look at a situation that someone is going through or thinking about going through, our words and

actions speak volumes to that situation.
There are people in our lives that look to
us to get our opinion and we can spoil
any faith by our response to that
situation. Whether it be a frown, a
shoulder shrug, a hmm, even a brow
turn, all of these can signal doubt or
unbelief. Our verbal response - no, I
don't think so, you can't, you shouldn't,
you won't be able, are you serious, can
all lead to doubt and unbelief.

Proverbs 18:21 Death and life are in the
power of the tongue: and they that love
it shall eat the fruit thereof.

We have to make sure we are seeking
God for answers to a certain situation
before we can give Godly wisdom to
someone in a situation where they really
don't know which way to go.

Deuteronomy 28:66 And thy life shall
hang in doubt before thee; and thou
shalt fear day and night, and shalt have
none assurance of thy life:

If you cannot be positive in a given
situation, make sure God is guiding you
before you speak into someone's life
regarding any situation. If we are
speaking with the wisdom of God and
the answer is a negative answer, there
will be peace at that moment instead of
doubt and unbelief. It is all in the
presentation of how the answer is given.

6. Giving finances

Luke 6:38 Give, and **it** shall be given unto you; good measure, pressed down, and shaken together, and running over, shall men give into your bosom. For with the same measure that ye mete withal it shall be measured to you again.

We can always be a help to someone financially. We do have to be careful how we give financially so that we don't always expect return from the individual

Proverbs 22:7 The rich ruleth over the poor, and the borrower is servant to the lender.

Financial help doesn't always mean money. You can help with paying bills for them, providing food, providing essential supplies, providing transportation to keep them from having to pay to get somewhere, helping with chores that they would have had to pay someone else. All of these examples lead to a financial gain for the individual you are helping out.

Money isn't everything, it is a tool that can be used just like time and effort. The money or other items you give to someone else to help their financial needs can be a seed for God to use in your own life. The important thing to remember when providing for someone else is that you do not forget your responsibility to God regarding the tithe. There are some people that are always helping others but never paying tithe to the local ministry that they attend.

Malachi 3:8 Will a man rob God? Yet ye have robbed me. But ye say, Wherein have we robbed thee? In **tithes** and offerings.

Financial giving is not just about helping others but also paying your tithe to the local ministry as well.

7. Giving fear

Luke 6:38 Give, and **it** shall be given unto you; good measure, pressed down, and shaken together, and running over, shall men give into your bosom. For with the same measure that ye mete withal it shall be measured to you again.

Have you ever snuck up behind someone and grabbed them just to see them jump? That jumping reaction is fear. Jumping in front of another car in traffic. Telling a scary story. These are all examples of fear.

Fear can be a weakness that keeps us from achieving the things we want in life. It leads to a lack of faith. Fear and faith cannot go together. When you are in fear, you are not sure of something. Meaning you don't know what or who something is. You don't understand what is going to happen next.

We as Christians have to approach situations where we are delivering bad or negative information, in a way that gives the individual faith and understanding instead of doubt and unbelief. Thoughts of – I don't know how or why or when, what is going to happen next, this can't be happening to me, the unknown factor in a given situation – these are all related to fear.

8. Giving victory

Luke 6:38 Give, and <u>it</u> shall be given unto you; good measure, pressed down, and shaken together, and running over, shall men give into your bosom. For with the same measure that ye mete withal it shall be measured to you again.

Some people might think, how can you give victory. It is very simple. Every time you provide something for someone that allows them to succeed in life or some type of project, that is victory. Once the need is met, it allows the individual to feel victorious. The most important thing here is that you are meeting the need according to God's will and not just what the individual thinks they need. We have to seek God to confirm that the need was met properly.

Luke 11:11 If a son shall ask bread of any of you that is a father, will he give him a stone? or if he ask a fish, will he for a fish give him a serpent?

There are situations we know what we want to give someone but we have to make sure it is the right solution to the situation.

Personal victory can be obtained by giving God more attention in every situation and not just a little time every day.

Hebrews 12:1-2

1. Wherefore seeing we also are compassed about with so great a cloud of witnesses, let us lay aside every weight, and the sin which doth so easily beset us, and let us run with patience the race that is set before us,

2. Looking unto Jesus the author and finisher of our faith; who for the joy that was set before him endured the cross, despising the shame, and is set down at the right hand of the throne of God.

Romans 8:37 Nay, in all these things we are more than conquerors through him that loved us.

1 Corinthians 15:57 But thanks be to God, which giveth us the victory through our Lord Jesus Christ.

God will guide us in every situation to achieve the victory if we will take the time to include Him in every situation.

Matthew 6:33 But seek ye first the kingdom of God, and his righteousness; and all these things shall be added unto you.

Proverbs 3:6 In all thy ways acknowledge him, and he shall direct thy paths

Joshua 1:8 This book of the law shall not depart out of thy mouth; but thou shalt meditate therein day and night, that thou mayest observe to do according to all that is written therein: for then thou shalt make thy way prosperous, and then thou shalt have good success.

Everything we do in life whether it be for ourselves or others can lead to either

victory or defeat. Always choose God's
way which leads to victory.

9. Giving time

Luke 6:38 Give, and **it** shall be given unto you; good measure, pressed down, and shaken together, and running over, shall men give into your bosom. For with the same measure that ye mete withal it shall be measured to you again.

This topic is probably the most important topic to make all the others work properly. If you do not spend time with God in prayer and the Word, He cannot help you improve your abilities to handle tough situations.

Matthew 6:33
But seek ye first the kingdom of God, and his righteousness; and all these things shall be added unto you.10

A particularly good example of time is Noah.   He spent 100 years building the ark. If you spend time with God and get used to listening to the Holy Spirit for wisdom and guidance, then He can actually change the way you approach different situations.

Luke 6:45

A good man out of the good treasure of his heart bringeth forth that which is good; and an evil man out of the evil treasure of his heart bringeth forth that which is evil: for of the abundance of the heart his mouth speaketh.

What this scripture says to me, garbage in garbage out – Word in Word out. The phrase I have heard all my life is you either have time or money. Use your time wisely. Make sure you have time to get with God, family and friends regularly. The most important time you can give is to make sure you are giving time to God to help you in your daily walk through life so you can help others in their time of need.

10. Seed Time and Harvest

With all giving, there is always a period of time when you may or may not see the results of your giving.

Genesis 8:22

^{22} While the earth remaineth, seedtime and harvest, and cold and heat, and summer and winter, and day and night shall not cease.

2 Corinthians, 9: 6-7

^{6} But this I say, He which soweth sparingly shall reap also sparingly; and he which soweth bountifully shall reap also bountifully.

^{7} Every man according as he purposeth in his heart, so let him give; not grudgingly, or of necessity: for God loveth a cheerful giver.

Galatians 6:7-9

[7] Be not deceived; God is not mocked: for whatsoever a man soweth, that shall he also reap.

,[8] For he that soweth to his flesh shall of the flesh reap corruption; but he that soweth to the Spirit shall of the Spirit reap life everlasting.

[9] And let us not be weary in well doing: for in due season, we shall reap if we faint not.

You can always count on this principle; you will reap what you sow it just may come back to you when you least expect it.   What this means is that in life, we know we are giving good things to others, but it seems like we never receive. If you take a closer look at your situation, you are most likely receiving due to your giving, but you just don't realize it is happening. Once we come to a realization that good things are coming in, we need to stop and give God the credit for all good things that come into our lives.

Following this same principle, when bad things are always happening to us, we need to take a strong look at our own life, and we will most likely see that we have been treating people the same way that some people are treating us.

As the old saying goes "What goes around, comes around."

Conclusion

In this book we have talked about several aspects of giving. It is vital to our survival that we make sure we are sharing our lives with others.

Acts 20:35 (KJV)

I have shewed you all things, how that so labouring ye ought to support the weak, and to remember the words of the Lord Jesus, how he said, It is more blessed to give than to receive.

Without giving there would be no receiving. Remember it does matter what you are giving whether it be physical, mental, emotional, or spiritual.

Luke 6:45 (KJV)

A good man out of the good treasure of his heart bringeth forth that which is good; and an evil man out of the evil treasure of his heart bringeth forth that which is evil: for of the abundance of the heart his mouth speaketh.

Actions lead to actions; words lead to words. Everything we do whether it be the words we use or the way we go about our daily lives, there will be corresponding actions. Throughout life, as long as we do not keep ourselves secluded and never see another person, there will always be opportunity to give and receive.

Our lives will always be full of opportunity to give. Make the best choice in each and every situation you face.

Romans 8:31(KJV)

 What shall we then say to these things? If God be for us, who can be against us?

Proverbs 3:6 (KJV)

In all thy ways acknowledge him, and he shall direct thy paths.